I0484770

CORPORATE SOCIAL RESPONSIBILITY

:: Author ::

ASHOKKUMAR D. PATEL

(M.COM)

PUBLISHED BY

The New Era International Publishing House
HQ. At & Po. Chaveli., Ta- Chansma,
Dist- Patan, North Gujarat, India, Asia.
www.iphouseindia.com

CORPORATE SOCIAL RESPONSIBILITY

First Publication: 21ST JANUARY, 2015

Copyright: Author

(c) ASHOKKUMAR D. PATEL

ISBN:- 978-15-08712-10-7

Price: Rs.750/- INDIA
$ 15 OUTSIDE INDIA

PUBLISHED BY

The New Era International Publishing House
HQ. At & Po. Chaveli., Ta- Chansma,
Dist- Patan, North Gujarat, India, Asia.
www.iphouseindia.com

Dedicated
to
my
Parents

An Overview of Contents

- **Corporate Social Responsibility - Meaning, Need and its Evolution**

- **Social Responsibilities of Organization Towards Customers**

- **Corporate Social Responsibility or Profits: The Debate**

- **CSR and Corporate Governance: Two Sides of the Same Coin**

- **A Win-Win Situation for All Stakeholders**

- **Environmental Destruction and Climate Change**

- **The Principles of the UN Global Compact**

- **What is the Bottom of the Pyramid and its Implications for Marketers**

- **Stockholder Management vs. Stakeholder Management**

Corporate Social Responsibility - Meaning, Need and its Evolution

The practice of CSR or Corporate Social Responsibility as a paradigm for firms and businesses to follow has evolved from its early days as a slogan that was considered trendy by some firms following it to the present day realities of the 21st century where it is no longer just fashionable but a business requirement to be socially responsible.

This evolution has been necessitated both due to the myriad problems that we as a race face which has changed the environment under which firms operate as well as a realization among business leaders that profits as the sole reason or raison d'être for existence can no longer hold good.

The reason why companies must look beyond profits is also due to the peculiar situation that humanity finds itself in the second decade of the 21st century. Given the political, economic, social and environmental crises that humans as a race are confronting, corporations have a role to play since they contribute the most to the economic well being of humanity and in turn influence the political and social trends.

Corporate Social Responsibility or CSR makes for eminent business sense as well when one considers the knock-on effect that social and environmental responsibility brings to the businesses. For instance, corporations exist in a symbiotic relationship with their environments (the term environment refers to all the components of the external environment and not to ecological environment alone) where their exchange with the larger environment determines to a large extent how well they do in their profit seeking endeavors.

The evolution of CSR as a concept dates back to the 1950's when the first stirrings of social conscience among management practitioners and theorists were felt. The writings of Keith Davis starting in the 1950's and continuing into the 1970's speak of the need for businesses to engage in socially responsible behavior and to ensure that society as a whole does not lose out in the process of profit making behavior by businesses. CSR as a concept was starting to be taken seriously by the time the 1970's dawned and through the tumultuous decade when big business and their minions were accused of several misdemeanors pertaining to rampant disregard for the environment and society as a whole.

One can trace the anxieties of activists and management theorists during this time as they feared that the rapacious behavior of businesses and corporations ought to be checked if a semblance of social responsibility was to be maintained. Of course, both sides started to stick to their positions and this resulted in the debate over CSR getting shriller during the 1980's. I conclude with two quotes that illustrate the need to think beyond the ordinary and at the same time remind ourselves of the responsibility we have towards succeeding generations: The first one by Albert Einstein where he said that "problems cannot be solved from the same level of consciousness that created them" and the second one which says that "We have not inherited the Earth. We have merely borrowed it from our children."

The Business Need for Corporate Social Responsibility

Corporate Social Responsibility or CSR makes for eminent business sense as well when one considers the knock-on effect that social and environmental responsibility brings to the businesses. For instance, corporations exist in a symbiotic relationship with their environments (the term environment refers to all the components of the external environment and not to ecological environment alone) where their exchange with the larger environment determines to a large extent how well they do in their profit seeking endeavours.

When one considers the fact that the RBV or the Resource Based View of the firm is all about how well the firm exists in harmony with its external environment and how this exchange of inputs and outputs with the environment determines the quality of its operations, it can be inferred that socially responsible business practices are indeed in the interest of the firm and the argument against imposing hidden social taxes on the firms by undertaking socially responsible business practices might not hold good in the current business landscape.

Indeed, the world since the days of Friedman has changed so much that socially responsible business practices ought to be the norm rather the exception and the various readings surveyed for this paper do seem to indicate that it is high time for businesses to engage in responsible behaviour. However, there is a tendency to treat CSR as yet another cost of business and hence be business like about the practice. So, mainstreaming the idea might not bring the desirable effect unless the media, the businesses, and the citizens themselves understand what is at stake and behave accordingly. Paying lip service or corporatizing the idea of CSR might not be the intended outcome of the proponents and the advocacy groups that promote this idea. Rather, a change in the mindset and attitude is what these groups have in mind when they push for socially responsible practices. It has been mentioned elsewhere that CSR as a concept and as a paradigm ought to be woven into the DNA of the corporations and when the very fabric resonates with the threads of social responsibility; the goals of conscious capitalism and compassionate corporations would be realized.

Hence, a cautionary finger wagging is due for those who believe that since the concept of CSR has been mainstreamed, they can relax in the knowledge that corporations would do the rest. Given the history of profit seeking and mercantilist behaviour where fads and ideas come and go but the very nature of the corporations mutates rather than undergoes a fundamental change, we still have some distance to cover before the goals of the idea of CSR are achieved. Further, we should not end up in a situation where the imperatives of the 21st century force corporations to change their behaviour. Instead, a voluntary mindset change is something that is better suited given the vast resources that corporations have and which they deploy to resist change and thwart those that push for legislation that aims to do so.

Importance of Corporate Social Responsibility

Corporate social responsibility allows organizations to do their bit for the society, environment, customers or for that matter stake holders.

Let us go through the importance of corporate social responsibility.

The term corporate social responsibility gives a chance to all the employees of an organization to contribute towards the society, environment, country and so on. We all live for ourselves but trust me living for others and doing something for them is a different feeling altogether. Bringing a smile to people's life just because your organization has pledged to educate the poor children of a particular village not only gives a sense of inner satisfaction but also pride and contentment. One should never forget the importance of society and environment in our lives. It is indeed high time when we also start thinking about people around us who are less privileged and fortunate than us. Corporate social responsibility gives an opportunity to organizations to work towards the betterment of the society and make it a better place to live.

Corporate social responsibility goes a long way in creating a positive word of mouth for the organization on the whole. Doing something for your society, stake holders, customers would not only take your business to a higher level but also ensure long term growth and success. Corporate social responsibility plays a crucial role in making your brand popular not only among your competitors but also media, other organizations and most importantly people who are your direct customers. People develop a positive feeling for a brand which takes the initiative of educating poor children, planting more trees for a greener environment, bringing electricity to a village, providing employment to people and so on. You really do not have to invest much in corporate social responsibility activities. Do not undertake CSR activities only to gain publicity but because you believe in the cause. There are many organizations which tap remote villages, some of which are even unheard as an initiative of corporate social responsibility.

Corporate social responsibility also gives employees a feeling of unparalleled happiness. Believe me, employees take pride in educating poor people or children who cannot afford to go to regular schools and receive formal education. CSR activities strengthen the bond among employees. People develop a habit of working together as a single unit to help others. Infact they start enjoying work together and also become good friends in due course of time. They also develop a sense of loyalty and attachment towards their organization which is at least thinking for the society. Who does not like to work with an organization where management is kind enough to take out time for the society and contribute in their own small way? Ask yourselves, when is the last time you did something for your society, customers, stake holders or environment? Corporate social responsibility also goes a long way in building a positive image of the brand. Trust me, your brand becomes a "common man's brand". People start believing in the brand and nothing can help you more than your customers trusting you and your brand. Positive word of mouth eventually helps to generate more revenues for the organization.

In today's scenario of cut throat competition, everyone is so occupied in chasing targets and handling the pressure at workplace that we actually forget that there is a world around us as well. Have you ever thought about those who can't even afford proper meal twice a day? If you can take some time out of your busy schedule, please try to visit a village once. You would be surprised to see how people manage their lives there. Corporate social responsibility in a way also plays a crucial role in the progress of the society, which would at the end of the day benefit us only.

Social Responsibilities of Organization Towards Employees

What is an organization without its employees? Nothing. Employees are said to be the true assets of an organization. Even the best of technology or best of infrastructure would not be of much use if employees do not perform up to the mark and are not satisfied with their current profiles.

As they say, "charity always begins at home". The first and the foremost responsibility of an organization towards its employees is to ensure that they are happy and satisfied with their jobs. It is unethical to treat employees as mere machines and expect them to work continuously for eight to nine hours at a stretch just because they are being paid. Do not treat your staff as labours. Management needs to ensure that individuals associated with their organization are actually enjoying what they are doing and also growing with time. Job profiles ought to be delegated equally as per expertise, knowledge and educational qualification of individuals so that no one is overburdened. Provide healthy working conditions to your employees. Assign proper workstations or cubicles for them to work comfortably and eventually deliver their level best. Everyone needs some amount of privacy and make sure your employees get the same; else soon they would be frustrated with their job and look for better opportunities.

Sit with your employees from time to time and try to find out whether they are happy with their job or not and if at all they are facing any problems in the system? It is the responsibility of the management to look after the safety of its employees. Ensure your office building is resistant to fire and earthquake. You can't play with the lives of so many individuals. Till the time an employee is on official duty, it becomes the responsibility of the organization to assist him/her in case of a medical emergency or other serious concern. If one of your engineers gets hurt at your site, it is your responsibility to immediately take him to the hospital and provide basic medical assistance.

Crisis can come anytime. If an employee asks for some advance from his/her salary, please do not say a blunt NO. Analyse the whole situation and find out how serious the whole issue is? He/she might need some money to treat his/her ailing father. It would be really inhuman to deny help during such circumstances. I don't think there should be much of a problem in this; after all, he is asking money from his own salary only. God forbid, if any of your employees dies, make sure you extend your sympathies and support to his/her family members to cope up with such an irreparable loss. Whenever your employees need your help, make sure you are there with them. A feeling of loyalty towards the organization comes only when the management treats all its employees as part of one big family and takes good care of them. Stand by each other not only during happy times but also sad moments. Remember; the fun is to enjoy not only the happiness but the challenges together.

Encourage employees to praise and appreciate each other.

Give them ample opportunities to show their talent. Provide them an environment where they can hone their skills with time. Problems arise when management puts a full stop on the growth of employees. Ask them to interchange roles, so that everyone gets to work on something new. Timely appraisals are important. It is the responsibility of the management to ensure that employees who are working really hard and showing progress are suitably rewarded. Incentives, cash prizes, bonuses go a long way in not only motivating the employees but also creating a healthy and positive ambience at the workplace.

Social Responsibilities of Organization Towards Customers

Let us go through some social responsibilities of an organization towards its customers.

Treat your customers as kings and do not think of them only when you have a pressure to meet your targets within the stipulated time frame. There are organizations that do not bother to touch base with their customers the whole month but are active only when they fall short of their targets and they have an appraisal in the coming month. Understand that a customer buys your products or services only when he/she trusts your brand and most importantly believes in you. Understand the needs and requirements of your clients. Find out as to why they need a particular product and how your product would benefit them. You need to build a strong relationship with your customers for them not only to remain your loyal clients but also bring more people along with them. It is the responsibility of the organization to give correct suggestions and feedbacks to customers. Avoid making fake promises and commitments which you yourself know are difficult to fulfil. What is the need of selling a mobile phone with just one day battery backup when the customer has specifically asked you for a handset with at least 3 days backup?

Never lie to your customers. It is foolish to cook false stories. Trust me, you will be caught. In today's world, where information is just a click away, everyone does his/her thorough research before purchasing something. Unnecessarily you will lose your respect in front of them. If you can't deliver something, please mention it clearly. They might not invest in that particular product but believe me, would definitely come back to you in near future just because you were honest and guided them correctly. It is pointless to badmouth your competitors.

Businesses dealing with customer's money need to be extra careful with clients. Make sure their money is invested in a right way and also multiples at a rate promised to them.

Do not run away with their money. It is one of the worst things you can do to your customers. It is your responsibility to take care of their hard earned money. Suggest them the right schemes and right plans as per their need. Do not just think of your own selfish targets and incentives. This way, you will definitely meet your targets once or twice but trust me not for a very long time. The moment, the customer knows that you have cheated on him/her; your game is over. He would neither come to you again nor recommend your brand to his friends or acquaintances.

Respect your customer's time. Do not decide the time and venue as per your availability and comfort. If the customer wants to meet you at 5 in the evening, make sure you are there on time. Neither reach too early nor too late. Do not keep your customers waiting. Do not forget that there are several options available in the market. Your loss is someone else's gain.

Organizations tend to forget their customers once the deal is done. After sales service is essential and ensures long term growth and profits for the organization. Make sure you are in touch with your customers after the deal as well if you wish to survive the cut throat competition. Do not ignore their calls once you have sold your product. If the customer is not satisfied with your product, it is your responsibility to replace it or provide a solution. Customer feedbacks are important and help you understand the satisfaction level of your esteemed customers and how you can make your product better in due course of time.

Corporate Social Responsibility(CSR) Leads to Increased Business Efficiency

In case corporations need some convincing to be done to adopt CSR, the model proposed by Young and Tilley (2006) where they list six criteria for corporate sustainability that not only contributes to the social responsibilities of the business but also improves the business efficiency. The latter if presented in a convincing manner would appeal to businesses since increased efficiency leads to greater cost savings as well as improved profit margins.

The six criteria discussed by Young and Tilley are eco-efficiency,socio-efficiency,eco-effectiveness,socio-Effectiven-ess and sufficiency and ecological equity. Taken together as a whole, these six criteria form an integrated model which corporations can follow for sustainable business practices and reap profits as well as be conscious in their business practices. The point here is that the motto that CSR pays in real economic terms ought to be broadcast far and wide and only when corporations realize the economic benefits of conscious capitalism would they embrace the paradigm of CSR wholeheartedly (Young & Tilley, 206, 411).

Given Friedman's injunction that the social responsibility of businesses is to make profits, if it can be shown that being socially responsible brings in profits, there can be no better business case for CSR.

This is realizable given the emerging research into CSR and business practices which throw up several connections between conscious capitalism and increased profits and the new "renaissance" in business thought and corporate behaviour ought to gladden the hearts of all CSR enthusiasts. Before concluding the paper, it would be pertinent to note that Friedman's article though cited widely might be a bit anachronistic for the imperatives of the 21st century and while the great professor was far sighted he could have not foreseen the complete breakdown of the neo classical model of economics that the Great Recession of 2008 has engendered.

Thus, while views such as that of Friedman's can be a good starting point as to debate the relative merits and demerits of social responsibility versus profits, to base the whole idea of CSR on his ideas alone would be doing a disservice to the non-linear, complex and interconnected world in which we live in and which demands appropriate out of the box solutions.

Corporate Social Responsibility or Profits: The Debate

In recent years, CSR or Corporate Social Responsibility has become the latest buzzword among the companies. This refers to the practice of the corporates in "giving back" to society in the form of programs that benefit the less privileged members of society. They can take the form of outreach programs that adopt schools; communities etc and provide funds for their upkeep as well as promote socially conscious business practices that lead to the betterment of society. This analyzes the statement, "the idea that the company's resources should be devoted to some cause other than making a profit is outrageous".

There is an ongoing debate over whether a firm should exist solely for making profits or whether it should pay heed to the social and environmental concerns that accompany the practice of Corporate Social Responsibility or CSR. The proponents of the view that a firm exists solely for making profit argue about the market being the final arbiter of allocating resources and point to the market as the place where incentives for allocating resources for social and environmental causes is to be found. The opponents of this view take the stand that everything cannot be left to the market and there needs to be a mechanism in place whereby the environmental and social causes need to be taken care of.

If we examine both sides of the debate as well as take into account superficial attempts by businesses to pay lip service to CSR, the first strand of thought that comes to mind is about the need for businesses to invest in CSR as a way of mitigating the deleterious effects of the industrial paradigm on the environment. The practice of CSR by industrial companies is in vogue these days because of the fact that they have contributed to polluting the environment. As Martha Nussbaum contends, "If this world is to be a decent world in the future, "we must acknowledge right now that we are citizens of one interdependent world, held together by mutual fellowship as well as the pursuit of mutual advantage, by compassion as well as self-interest, by a love of human dignity in all people, even when there is nothing we have to gain from cooperating with them"

Hence, in this interconnected and flat world there is a need for concerted action by the businesses to take steps that would alleviate the pressing issues of the day. However, the opponents of this view are some of the multinationals themselves as can be seen from the following excerpt, "Thus the central theoretical and practical question in the discussion of corporate social responsibility is whether it remains a voluntary choice of the business or should be ensured through formal control".

The point here is that CSR is being enforced rather than voluntarily embraced. This fact alone makes it clear that businesses by themselves do not contribute to CSR and that they have to be regulated to do so.

Green Washing, Corporate Spin and CSR

As for superficial attempts to practice CSR, the term "green washing" gives an instance of how the aims of CSR are subverted. Green Washing refers to the practice of the corporate spin employed by a company in declaring itself to promoting environmentally friendly policies whereas in reality, the company does not live up to the rhetoric. This is a practice that should be avoided and as noted in the above sections, some companies usually "walks the talk" and there have been no instances of the company indulging in practices that it otherwise repudiates in public. As the Corporate governance council is responsible for overseeing the activities of its CSR and ethical standard compliance, it is the nodal committee for ensuring that there is no "spin" on the business practices.

The opponents of CSR argue about the recessionary times and how difficult it is for them to practice CSR when the focus is on cutting costs and improving the bottom line. In this context, it is pertinent to consider the following excerpt from a Business Week article, "At the root of these innovations is a corporate philosophy that strives for some kind of good beyond mere profits. At the same time, goodness can be good for the bottom line, too. At a time of financial crisis, climate change, vast economic disparities, and pandemics, the existence of companies trying to right wrongs and fix things is certainly soothing"

Till now, this has considered the opposing viewpoints about CSR and as can be seen from the "slant" of the quotations that We have selected as well as our opinions, it is our firm belief that a firm does indeed exist for making things other than profit and hence, the practice of CSR ought to be enforced rather than merely suggested. We live in times where the author James Martin has pointed to the dangers inherent in our current paradigm and raised the point about how the central challenge of our time is to ensure that we transition to a new paradigm. Hence, the need of the hour is for businesses and regulators alike to embrace CSR and the notion that a firm exists solely for making profits belongs to the old paradigm.

In conclusion, it is our opinion that companies and businesses work together with the governmental agencies to promote sustainable practices and alleviate the severe environmental and social problems that are besetting us and in this respect, the firms should indeed look beyond their bottom line and have a social component in their accounting statements as a means of measuring the environmental and social impact of their businesses. It is worth remembering that we have not inherited the earth but merely borrowed it from our children. Hence, we do have a duty to make the world a habitable place for future generations and focus on sustainability instead of destruction.

The Practice of Corporate Social Responsibility (CSR) around the World

The last dealt with how Corporate Social Responsibility (CSR) evolved from its early beginnings in the 1950's to a full-fledged business imperative by the second decade of the 21st century. If we turn our gaze to the geographical evolution of the concept i.e. the way in which businesses in different regions across the world adopted and implemented the idea, we find that there is no uniformity in the timeline nor there is a consensus on what actually constitutes CSR among businesses in different parts of the world. For instance, CSR as a concept found its feet more in Europe than in the US though the latter was responsible for its early initiation into business literature.

The fact that the "green consciousness" and the "green movement" secured major gains in Europe meant that companies and firms in the continent were more amenable towards CSR than their counterparts in the US. However, in recent years, there has been a "levelling off" with the body polity in the US recognizing the need for businesses to be held accountable and hence shaking off the long inertia that enveloped them during the time Europe was making rapid strides in implementing CSR.

This has led to the mainstreaming of the idea of CSR to the extent that we have reached a point (in the West) where CSR is a business imperative in the same way taking care of the workforce is. The policies and programs that have been launched by many firms routinely include their commitment towards CSR and their affirmation of the need to be socially responsible. However, the other continents like Asia and Latin America were lagging behind for a long time in even recognizing that businesses have a social responsibility. Though this might seem primitive or Luddite to say that businesses need have absolutely no responsibility towards society, the fact that many firms and businesses in these regions practiced a variety of capitalism that was unique to those countries and which included a certain inbuilt social conscience.

Hence, while it cannot be said that these regions and countries were left behind totally, the concept as it is perceived in the West was not being practiced here. Many commentators in these countries initially dismissed the idea of CSR as an imperialist construct and something that is a luxury much in the same way that early adopters in US and Europe faced these accusations. However, in recent decades, countries like India and Brazil have indeed taken the lead in making businesses adopt policies that are socially responsible, environmentally conscious, compassionate in their human dimensions and thrifty in their use of natural resources. The United Nations has had a significant role to play in universal acceptance of the idea of CSR with their promotion of the "Global Compact" to which various countries are signatories. This global compact binds the signatories to universally accepted principles of social responsibility which the businesses in those countries ought to follow and which is tracked for implementation.

Role of the Media in Championing CSR

Till now have focused on how corporations need to embrace CSR (Corporate Social Responsibility) as a business imperative. The emphasis mostly was on how there are business needs to adopt CSR and it is high time the corporations became socially conscious. we look at the role of the Media in championing CSR. Indeed, the media have a huge role to play in how CSR is broadcast to the world at large. It is simply not enough for corporations to do their bit for social causes. They must also let the world know so that others are inspired and they set an example for others to follow. Of course, we are not talking about "advertising" CSR per se because then it would fall into the category of the corporations trumpeting their achievements like they would do when they launch new products.

On the other hand, what we are saying is that they must follow the example of ITC and Vedanta that have created brilliant ads that portray their values and showcase the excellent work that they have been doing. There are other companies like Shell that have come out with innovative ways to reach out to the people about their CSR initiatives.

Apart from creating appealing and conscious ads, corporations must enlist the cooperation and support of media in spreading awareness about CSR to the people at large. In the final analysis, CSR is all about helping society look beyond profits and hence the media (which is a guardian of public good) has a stellar role to play in this endeavor.

The media can be used to seek volunteers from the society or the specific places where the corporations are launching their CSR initiatives. Further, they can be used to pertaining to the values and the mission of the company in promoting CSR. An excellent example of this relationship is the way Infosys is covered in the media. There are very few which do not mention the respect and the adulation that Infosys commands from the Indian public at large and this has been made possible because of adroit media coverage. The way in which the social initiatives undertaken by Infosys have been covered in the media speaks volumes about how well the company has managed its media coverage.

Apart from this, the media can also act as a conscience keeper by constantly reminding corporations about the need to give back to society and to look beyond profits. Internationally, The Guardian Newspaper has been at the forefront of demanding accountability and transparency from the corporations. In India, The Hindu does a good job of publishing articles and editorials that exhort the corporations to be socially conscious. Finally, the media can also take a critical view of the CSR programs that a corporation claims to run and it can ensure that the corporation is not indulging in "Green Washing" which is the case where a corporation pretends to follow CSR but in reality does not do so.

Advocacy Groups and Corporate Social Responsibility (CSR)

We have seen how corporations need to embrace CSR as a paradigm if the challenges of the 21st century have to be met. We have also examined the role of the media in championing CSR.

In this, we look at how Advocacy Groups and Pressure Groups like Greenpeace and Media Lens along with other NGO's (Non Governmental Organizations) have a prominent role in advocating corporations to follow socially conscious policies and programs. These advocacy groups exist to monitor how well the corporations are adhering to socially conscious norms and the extent to which they are following business practices that do good for society. The way in which Greenpeace champions socially responsible capitalism is a case in point. There are other pressure groups like India Resource Center (formerly Corp Watch) that are actively monitoring the implementation of socially responsible business practices.

The case of the Coca Cola plant in Plachimada, Kerala is instructive for the notable successes that advocacy groups have had in pressurizing the Coca Cola Company to desist from drawing excess groundwater as well as prevent it from desalinating the surrounding areas. This is a much quoted and oft cited case where the advocacy groups and the NGO's like India Resource Center actively participated in filing lawsuits against Coca Cola for its transgressions. The point here is not to belittle the companies but to highlight the point that advocacy groups have an important role to play in persuading and monitoring companies in their CSR programs.

Any country needs to have watchdogs to keep track of the entities that make up the body polity. In the same way that courts are the custodians of the law and act as a check on the executive, **the advocacy groups act like watchdogs of corporate behavior**. Hence, any deviation in corporate behavior is actively recorded and published by these groups. Of course, there are many NGO's that partner with corporations as well and the examples of Janagraha and CRY (Child Relief and You) are the prominent ones. So, there are both sides to the coin where advocacy groups act to prevent corporates from indulging in socially irresponsible behavior as well as those that work with companies in implementing CSR programs.

There are many companies that have their own foundations and trusts that undertake CSR programs. For instance, the Infosys Foundation and the TATA Trust are examples of where the corporation-advocacy relationship is actualized in practice. Many of these foundations and trusts are staffed with people from the social service field and hence they have a mandate of their own. Finally, whether an advocacy group partners with corporations or monitors and fights irresponsible behavior, it is clearly the case that such groups have a vital role to play in upholding the social norms that businesses have to follow. Only when there is a healthy balance between the corporations and the advocacy groups can genuine CSR programs succeed. In conclusion, CSR is something that needs to come from the heart of companies and so they are the final custodians of whether the programs that they undertake are conscientious.

Practicing Socially Responsible Practices Internally

In modules, we have seen how companies need to adopt CSR as a business need and imperative. The role of media and advocacy groups was discussed as well. we turn to a crucial but often neglected aspect of a company's social responsibility i.e. the need to be socially conscious with its own employees and other stakeholders. Practicing CSR for external consumption and as a means to look good in the eyes of society would amount to nothing if the internal environment of the organization is driven by harassment, excessive coercion and intolerance towards diversity. In such cases, the company would be hypocritical in its approach if it says that it is socially responsible. There are many examples of companies that have failed to set right their environments though outwardly they claim that they are socially responsible.

If we take the example of Infosys that has been witnessing a high turnover of employees in recent years because of harsh working conditions, we find that it is the classic example of a company that does not practice what it preaches.

We certainly do not want to belittle Infosys because its achievements are legendary. Just that we would like to draw attention to the fact that the sexual harassment case involving its ex-sales head Phaneesh Murthy is representative of the fact that companies need to be tolerant towards diversity internally as well if they are said to be socially responsible. Of course, the aftermath of the case was handled well which speaks volumes about the maturity of the organizational processes. However, the larger point is that companies need to encourage and tolerate diversity if they are to win public approval and show that they really care about social responsibility.

The recent instances of companies having issues with labor management and which otherwise follow CSR is another instance of the fact that it is high time these companies followed the adage: Charity Begins at Home. Some examples are the lockdown of the Maruti Plant in Manesar, India and internationally, the troubles that Apple is facing in China because of discriminatory, oppressive and unsafe working conditions in its factories in that country. Since both these companies are reputed to be socially conscious, the point that they need to set their own house in order first need not be belabored.

The fact of the matter is that bad press arising out of such instances of misconduct hits any company hard and more so if the overly stated goal of the company is to be socially responsible. Hence, the overriding conclusion is that companies need to be mature and realize that they must practice socially conscious policies with their workforce as well. Simply launching charitable trusts and foundations when the workplace environment is vitiated does not serve the company's purpose. In fact, it does more harm than good as the critics would use these instances as an opportunity to launch attacks on the company and its policies thereby weakening the trust that the company enjoys with consumers.

Examples of Companies with good Corporate Social Responsibility

, we have discussed the pitfalls of companies not managing their CSR strategies appropriately resulting in poor press coverage as well as outrage among activists and degraded public opinion. we concentrate on the positive aspect of how companies have managed their CSR strategies well and are reaping the benefits of doing so. The first company that comes to mind as a beacon of good corporate governance is the Indian IT industry bellwether, Infosys. Indeed, Infosys is one of the companies that has set benchmarks for other companies not only in India but all over the world in the way corporate governance and social responsibility are handled and projected to the outside world. The point here is that companies not only need to walk the talk for CSR but also broadcast their achievements to the world at large.

Another company that has done an exceptional job of portraying itself as a good corporate citizen is the **TATA group** in India and The Body Shop (formerly owned by Anita Roddick) company in the United States.

While these two companies are at different ends of the spectrum as far as their product lines and lines of business are concerned, the public perceives these companies favourably mainly due to the visionary leaders that have led these companies as well as the reputation that has been established through decades of doing the right thing. Taken together with Infosys and companies like Sony Ericsson, these corporations reap the benefits of being good corporate citizens in terms of increased revenues and top of the mind brand recall by dint of being model corporate citizens.

The key take away from this discussion is that companies do gain tangible and intangible benefits by practising CSR and by projecting an image of good governance and social responsibility to the external world. Of course, we have seen how companies resort to "Green

Washing" and spin to project something which does not exist fully or partially. The point about these examples is that these companies not only pursue socially and environmentally responsible strategies but also make it a point to be on cordial terms with all the stakeholders (the suppliers, governmental agencies, employees, consumers and society at large) which translates into measurable and immeasurable benefits to these companies.

Finally, being a good corporate citizen brings its own benefits to the companies. For instance, it is common to find leaders from these companies sitting on various boards and advisory committees which speak volumes about the high esteem in which they are held. This translates into instant recognition and a "halo" effect which for all practical purposes is like the adulation that rock stars and sports personalities receive from the people. The point here is that good corporate behavior is rewarded at some point or the other and hence, companies must seek to do well and do the right thing always. While not preaching, some of these companies also help other companies in actualizing their visions for society and by being transformational change agents as well as catalysts for CSR.

In conclusion, CSR as a business imperative must not be accepted grudgingly or half heartedly. Instead, it must be practiced with full vigor and straight from the heart passion and this certainly helps the companies in the long run. After all, business is not all about the next quarter only.

The Bhopal Disaster and its Aftermath as a Case Study in Misapplication of CSR

In previous we have discussed how Corporate Social Responsibility (CSR) as a business imperative is no longer a luxury and instead, it has become a necessity. We have also discussed how companies can no longer afford to pay lip service to CSR and the time has come to take the concept seriously. Indeed, the stakes are high for companies that chose to ignore societal concerns as evidenced in the way companies that have ridden roughshod over social obligations have found to their consternation that the awakening public consciousness demands answers from the companies. This discusses the specific case of the disaster in the Union Carbide Plant in Bhopal, India as an instance of how the disaster itself and the way in which the aftermath of the disaster are being handled is a classic case of misapplication of the concept of Social Responsibility.

This does not go into the details of the industrial accident. Instead, what this discusses is how Dow Corporation (the current owner of the plant) has sought to shirk responsibility and is being pilloried by the media and the people at large for the way in which its brazen attempts to override societal obligations is costing the company.

We need not look further than the recent brouhaha over Dow being one of the sponsors of the upcoming 2012 Olympics in London and the negative press that has been generated because of the worldwide protests by activists and civil society groups. Indeed, it has now become the norm for popular opinion to turn against Dow whenever the Bhopal Incident is mentioned.

Further, there has been outrage over the way in which the Public Relations for the Dow Company have been handled with many critics pointing to the callous disregard that the company has for public opinion of its handling the fallout from the Bhopal Disaster. Notwithstanding the claims of the company that it does not have anything to do with the disaster as the previous owner of the plant is responsible, it is a basic fact in the corporate world that adequate due diligence has to be done by companies when they acquire other companies and in this case, Dow cannot evade responsibility since it very well knew the antecedents of the Union Carbide Corporation which it acquired.

Finally, the way in which Dow refuses to accept social responsibility and exhibit good corporate behavior by reaching out to the victims of the disaster speaks volumes about the way in which the company is reneging on its social responsibility. Hence, in this case at least, CSR should be something that Dow ought to practice fully and in good faith if it can claim that its conscience is clear. It is the case that Dow bears some social responsibility and it cannot turn away from this. The case of the handling of the aftermath of the disaster is a very real test for governments and corporate watchdogs all around the world in making companies accountable and socially responsible.

In conclusion, it would be an understatement to say that Dow mishandled its social responsibility. Indeed, it can be said that the company is in fact behaving in a way that disregards commonsense notions of corporate responsibility and it does not take an expert in CSR to realize that Dow ought to be made to take its social responsibility seriously.

The Practice of Corporate Governance is as Important as Social Responsibility

we have seen how CSR is practiced by companies and how the present times with their myriad challenges need companies to be socially and environmentally responsible. we look at how companies first need to shore up their internal governance mechanisms before turning to the outside world to display their social concern. The focus here is that unless companies set their own house in order, social responsibility cannot be achieved. We need not turn farther than the example of Satyam Computers (now merged with Tech Mahindra) wherein the company was indeed practicing CSR but internally the corporate governance structures were so rotten that the scam once it came to light was mind boggling.

This example shows that good corporate governance is a prerequisite to CSR. For instance, the various charitable trusts and the 108 Ambulance services that were being sponsored by Satyam ran aground once the scandal became known to the public.

This shows the need for good internal governance first and then practicing CSR as otherwise there would be issues of credibility and trust. The other example is that of the Enron Corporation which in itself was engaged in dubious internal accounting and shady business practices. No wonder that the shareholders and other stakeholders who invested in Enron were left flabbergasted with the extent of the corporate mis-governance.

The implications of this are clear. Corporate leaders ought to concentrate first on providing sound governance and fair business practices. Then they should look towards practicing CSR. The point here is that companies ought to walk the talk where CSR is concerned and hence, they must first be internally and externally conscionable. This can be actualized by following transparent accounting, oversight over business practices and regular auditing of the company's procedures and processes. Only when whistleblowers are encouraged and there are mechanisms for grievance redressal can there be good corporate governance. And only when there is good corporate governance can there be effective concern for society.

The key take away from this discussion is that companies must actualize their vision for society by following sound business practices which would go a long way in ensuring reputational benefits and top of the mind recall. For instance, companies like Infosys are known for their good corporate governance world over and hence society looks up to them for guidance and direction whenever ethical and social concerns are discussed. Further, these companies set standards for others to follow and hence are considered benchmarks on which corporate governance ought to be measured.

It is apparent that good corporate governance is the first step towards keeping employees, shareholders and other stakeholders happy and hence is the first step towards practicing CSR. When companies behave with integrity and trust they engender confidence among the stakeholders which translates into socially responsible business practices. In conclusion, good corporate governance is becoming more important by the day and with the spate of scandals that have rocked major corporations in recent times, it is imperative that companies follow sound business practices.

Changing Times Need Changing Approach towards CSR

The world is changing before our eyes and whether one actively participates in that or is a bystander, the changes affect all of us. This is true in the business world as well where resource crunch, power outages and labor unrest means that companies have to take extra precautions to survive the present times. When one looks at the worldwide scenario, it is full of economic gloom and forecasts of things getting worse. In this scenario, it is no longer the case that sustainability and corporate responsibility are just catchphrases or things that the companies can do at their leisure. Instead, they have become paradigms in their own right which must be followed if the companies and the environment that sustains them have to transition to a new paradigm.

The point here is that corporate behavior must change with the changing times and hence excessive exploitation of resources along with causing environmental damage would be severely punished. In this context, it is worth noting that companies around the world have adopted corporate responsibility into their business strategies.

Further, the United Nations has made several corporations around the world signatories to their Global Compact. This Global Compact is a set of principles that bind companies to social responsibility and encourage them to adopt sustainable business practices. With the Global Compact and the Millennium Development Goals set by the UN, corporates around the world have incentives to participate in creating a better world.

The ongoing global economic crisis has made sustainability a key parameter as the excesses of the capitalist era precipitated the crisis and catalyzed the movement towards sustainability.

Hence, the WTO (World Trade Organization) as well as the IMF and World Bank have incorporated sustainability into their mandates and are actively encouraging and goading the corporations around the world to adopt corporate social responsibility. In China and India, the severe power shortages and labor unrest has forced many companies to address social responsibility which along with the cost to the environment because of pollution has led to severe penalties from the regulators.

Taking all these factors into account, there is now a widespread acceptance of the fact that corporate social responsibility is no longer an extra business practice but a necessity. The winds of change are sweeping across the world and it is high time the corporations realized the inevitability of change and transition to a new paradigm. Unless companies learn to do with less and do not cause damage to the environment, there is no way in which humanity is going to survive. This message must be sent loud and clear by bodies like the UN, WTO, IMF and World Bank and it is only when there is a realization of this aspect that effective and deep actions can be taken. We have to realize that change takes time and so there must be patience with the change process.

Finally, this is a time for visionary leadership and sagacious wisdom from the top CEO's and management of corporations. Without the mandate coming from the top, it is difficult to actualize change and create an environment where the future generations have something to look forward to instead of being pessimistic. This is the central challenge of our times and it needs to be seen how far the present leadership of major corporations follows the Global Compact and the Sustainability Principles set out by the UN.

CSR and Corporate Governance: Two Sides of the Same Coin

We discussed how effective corporate governance is essential for a well functioning economy and how the practice of good corporate governance is the lubricant that greases the machine of the corporate world. We had also discussed how the practice of corporate social responsibility or CSR is a step in the direction of effective corporate governance. The point here is that companies that practice good corporate governance are also those that are socially and environmentally responsible.

Being a good corporate citizen means that companies have to be internally well governed and externally responsible.

In other words, CSR and corporate governance are two sides of the same coin. The implication here is that unless corporates practice good governance they are unlikely to have a social conscience and hence the first step towards CSR is through practicing the art of effective corporate governance.

The role of the board of directors and the management is especially critical since they are the final arbiters of the actions of the companies. The buck stops with them and hence they have to ensure that the companies that they represent are run effectively and at the same time take into account the social and the environmental concerns. It is not without basis that companies like Dow Chemicals and Pfizer are routinely accused of malfeasance and unethical behavior since they have outstanding liabilities as a result of their past actions. On the other hand, companies like Unilever and Infosys are often held up as examples of the way in which effective corporate governance can be practiced. The choice for other companies is clear: either they set their own house in order and comply with social and environmental norms or they run the risk of a sullied image among the investors and the consumers at large.

The next aspect is that the employees and the stakeholders including the shareholders have an important function to perform as far as the twin objectives of good corporate governance and the practice of CSR are concerned. Since effective corporate governance means that internal democracy and external responsibility go hand in hand, all the stakeholders have a duty towards the company to persuade the management to follow ethical and social norms of doing business. This is a manifestation of what has been called shareholder activism and stakeholder involvement which means that the entire stakeholder and the shareholders can exercise power over the actions of the board and the management to steer them towards the practice of good corporate governance and CSR.

Finally, the pressure groups and the consumers at large can vote with their wallets and their unrelenting focus on the actions of the corporates to bring about effective corporate governance. As the cliché goes, charity begins at home and hence corporates need to ensure that their internal governance models are robust before they embark on CSR. In conclusion, there is a mass awakening of sorts that is happening with society at large waking up to the need for corporates to be ethical and socially responsible and conscious. Hence, no corporate can afford to ignore the telltale signs of consumer and stakeholder focus on these aspects.

The Costs and Consequences of Climate Change for Business and Society

What is Climate Change and its Consequences

Climate change or the phenomenon of deviations in climate patterns from the norm is having a noticeable and immediate effect on the world. What was a warning in the 1970s and a gradual trend in the last decades of the 20th century has turned into an immediate impact factor on the ecosystems and the climate of the world. For instance, the recent cloudbursts, flooding, and landslides in India are being blamed on extreme precipitation of rainfall in some areas, which leads to the kind of events that we have seen over the last month. It is no longer the case that we can deny the effects of climate change that manifest themselves as extreme heat, extreme cold, and global warming that result in the rising of mean temperatures across the world and the rise in sea levels threatening the existence of several coastal areas. In other words, climate change has gone mainstream and hence, it cannot be ignored any longer.

The Costs of Climate Change on Businesses and Society

The effects of climate change on businesses can be seen in the way companies in the oil and gas sector, manufacturing, and resources along with those that are dependent on seasonal aspects like agriculture have to factor in the effects of climate change into their operations. For instance, drought caused due to extreme heat and lack of rainfall can make the agri-based companies suffer losses, as is the case when extreme precipitation and rainfall can cause flooding of the fields or the area under cultivation leading to losses. Further, businesses have to be prepared for wars between nations that manifest as a result of climate change or "climate wars" as they are called. These climate wars happen because of migrations of people from regions that are inhospitable to those regions that are relatively better off. This is happening in Africa where because of the effects of climate change, forced migration and extreme weather is causing many countries to fight with each other. Apart from that, climate wars can also result because of scarcity of water in particular regions, which make them invade or encroach into other countries in search of arable land for cultivation.

Are we beyond the Point of No-Return ?

The point to be noted about climate change is that incidents like the melting of the Polar Ice Caps or the melting of the glaciers in hilly areas can cause damage to ecosystems and precipitate calamities in the regions affected. As we have mentioned earlier, the recent incidents like the one in India and the drought in the US along with Hurricane Sandy in New York are all manifestations of climate change. These events can cause dislocations in societies and cause Black Swan Events (events with low probability, but high impact) which can cause havoc in the financial markets as well as having a noticeable economic impact on the countries. The key aspect here is that we are already past the point of no return and hence, we cannot stop the effects of climate change but can ensure that we manage them better.

Reducing our Carbon Footprint

The way to manage the impact of climate change would be to minimize the carbon footprint or the carbon emissions per head. This is an indicator, which tells us how many tons of carbon dioxide that we are emitting because of our vehicles, our transport, and our work and living conditions. As mentioned earlier, we are at a stage where we cannot reverse climate change but can mitigate it. Therefore, we should minimize our consumption of oil, make our offices and our homes eco-friendly, and in general, desist from using too many resources that need energy in one form or the other. These are some of the practical steps that we can take to minimize the impact of climate change. Finally, we must prepare for lives that are symbolized as "After the Car" which means that we need to move to a sustainable form of living and working as opposed to overconsumption and overuse of carbon emitting methods.

What are Offshore Tax Havens and their Uses and Misuses ?

What are Offshore Tax Havens ?

In recent years, there has been a lot of media interest in Offshore Tax Havens or countries where the global companies can base their offices as well as route their investments into emerging markets from offshore subsidiaries. **To define offshore tax havens, they are countries where there is no tax on the profits earned by the companies based in their jurisdiction**. For instance, if a company is located in the Cayman Islands, Luxembourg, or the Isle of Mann apart from Mauritius, it need not pay any taxes on its profits earned by it. Hence, the term offshore tax haven because it is located away from traditional centers of business and because the tax breaks offered to the companies are like a haven for them. This means that if a multinational wants to setup its headquarters in one of the many tax havens, it not only gets its profits without taxes but it can also invest in mainland countries where it can claim that since it is headquartered in an offshore tax haven, it need not pay tax in the mainland as well.

The Misuse of Tax Havens

It has been estimated that the global economy foregoes more than a Trillion Dollars in taxes every year because of the tax havens. Further, there are agreements between the offshore tax havens and the mainland countries on double tax avoidance, which means that both countries sign an agreement that declares that if a company is being taxed in one country, it need not pay the same tax in the other country. However, in practice the double tax avoidance works to the advantage of the companies as more often than not the offshore tax havens levy a negligible tax on the company is leading to these companies avoiding paying taxes in the mainland country. Of course, disputes arise because of these provisions as was seen in the case involving Vodafone and the Government of India. The Income Tax department in India held that Vodafone was avoiding taxes on its acquisitions in India because it claimed that the investments were routed through Mauritius. On the other hand, Vodafone contested the tax bill strongly and the case went to the Supreme Court that ruled in the IT department's favor. It is another matter that the dispute is now being arbitrated at different levels and a final decision is still pending.

Strong Opposition to Tax Havens

The reason why many activists and experts voice concern over the offshore tax havens is that thought they promote globalization and free trade; they skew the incentives in favor of tax avoidance rather than productive contributions. Considering the fact that the governments of the world need taxes to actualize social welfare, offshore tax havens indeed work against social justice. The situation in the UK is more alarming as it has been found that most British and Multinational companies in the UK take advantage of the offshore tax havens and avoid paying tax altogether. Moreover, they also resort to what is known as transfer pricing, which means that they quote different prices in the target country and different prices in the tax havens to exploit the loopholes in the system. This again leads to a situation where even the meager amounts of tax on the operations of the firms in the UK are largely avoided. Further, social activists also point to the scope for criminal activities and money laundering that these tax havens offer to their clients. This is the reason that there has been a concerted effort by activists in recent times to force governments to act tough against tax havens.

Concluding Remarks

Finally, corporates have a duty towards society and this is the reason that they must not exploit the system to their advantage. This is also the reason why governments of the world must come together to plug the loopholes and the lacunae in the laws to ensure that corporates pay taxes like anybody else.

Catch Them Young and Watch Them Grow: CSR Initiatives in Primary and Secondary Education

CSR Initiatives in Primary and Secondary Education

CSR or Corporate Social Responsibility initiatives can extend to the realm of primary and secondary education. This entails close engagement and involvement of corporates in the schools, colleges, and universities where the corporate provide for funds, training, and associated programs with a view to educate the future workforce on how the corporate world works and the expectations from the future employees. It has been found that in many developing countries, there is a disconnect between the education that the students receive during their graduate programs and the expectations from them when they join the workforce. Indeed, it has been estimated that out of the millions of graduates in countries like China and India, only 10-20 percent are employable meaning that the rest do not have language, comprehension, verbal, and aptitude based skills to find gainful and meaningful employment. This is the reason why many industry bodies in these countries have taken it upon themselves to reach out to the colleges and universities and impart skill based training programs so that the students upon graduation can be employed and be employable.

A Win-Win Situation for All Stakeholders

The other aspect about corporate outreach in schools, colleges, and universities has to do with building a brand image among the future workforce. Not only does this help the corporates in recruiting potential employees who are the best and the brightest but would help them in inculcating a sense of what it takes to succeed in the corporate world upon graduation. Indeed, as part of the brand building exercise, the corporates can also provide for funds to the schools, colleges, and universities so that the equipment and the technology for vocational skill building can be provided for. In other words, the corporates can combine their CSR activities with brand building and this would be a double whammy that would benefit all stakeholders in the process. Apart from this, the corporates can also fund needy students so that they can complete their education. Further, it has become the practice for many corporates to institute leadership awards in business schools that are targeted at women leaders, future leaders and potential leaders so that the leadership skills can be honed right from the time the students start their education. This is the case with many business schools in the west where leading companies often give out leadership awards to those whom they consider potential leaders.

Industry Academia Collaboration is good for alignment of objectives

The third aspect about CSR initiatives in primary and secondary education is that they help the collaboration between the industry and the academia, which would result in close alignment of what the corporates want and what the universities teach. In other words, in many universities, there is a disconnect between the research undertaken in the universities and the emerging trends that industry and the corporates are handling. This disconnect can be remedied by close engagement and collaboration between the researchers and the faculty in the universities so that there is alignment of objectives between these stakeholders. Further, by instituting chairs and fellowships, the corporates can benefit from increased exposure and involvement with academia. This is the case in most of the leading universities in the west that have dedicated programs that are funded by corporates.

Concluding Remarks: Catch Them Young and Watch Them Grow

Finally, the combination of CSR and brand building as well as funding and working closely with primary and secondary education is a win-win situation for all stakeholders. As the title of this states, it is better to catch them young and watch them grow. In other words, identifying future leaders, nurturing talent and incubating ideas right from school and college is a noble initiative that brings in good rewards for the students and the corporates and helps in aligning the objectives between academia and corporates.

If We Do Not Change Direction, We Will End Up in the Same Place that the Crisis is Taking Us

Confronting a No-Growth Economy

The main problem facing the global economy is that growth has stalled and excessive money printing has led to inflation.

There is a saying which goes something like this, if you do not change direction, you are likely to end up in the same place that your life is taking you when you are in a crisis. This means that in times of crisis, there is an urgent need to reverse gears and change directions or otherwise, we will end up in an economic abyss. Especially when one considers the fact that, the policymakers all over the world have been unable to "solve" the present crisis, which means that unless we take radical steps to confront and conquer the present crisis, we will end up being victims of it instead of coming out strong from the crisis. Moreover, the no growth economy has meant that speculation is rampant and when one trades in paper without any backing of tangible assets, eventually the paper one is trading in becomes worthless because it does not have an intrinsic value leading to a crash of historic proportions.

Un-Sustainability of the Present Economic Model

The second problem that is staring at us in the face is that the current economic paradigm is dead and there is nothing to replace it. Indeed, the intellectual bankruptcy is so high that all experts are unable to arrive at a solution to the present economic model that has failed miserably. The only way out of the mess that we find ourselves in is through sustainable economics, which means that the days of infinite growth are over, and that we have to confront the inconvenient fact that infinite growth is not possible in a finite world. In other words, the sooner we adjust ourselves to the new economic realities of resource-constrained growth, the better it would be for us to start living within our means and not have fantasies of double-digit growth, which is not coming to us anytime soon. The point here is that an economic model based on too much debt and a fast depleting resource base needs more growth to sustain itself and when the growth is not appearing anywhere, the only way out would be for us to change the direction in which we are heading and instead, lead our lives in a manner that is sustainable.

Environmental Destruction and Climate Change

The third and an often-overlooked problem that the world is facing is that our current economic model has caused so much environmental damage that it might be too late to save the environment. The only other option would be to try to slow down the irreversible processes of climate change and global warming so that we might at least be spared of the worst consequences. As has been pointed out repeatedly if we do not change direction, we are headed down the path of disaster. When changing direction becomes difficult, we can at least slow down the vehicle so that we can limit the damage to ourselves and to our future generations. The point here is that many of the problems that the world is facing are beyond the point of no return and hence, unless urgent steps are taken, we might be just about managing to join the long list of species that have become extinct because of our unsustainable ways of living.

Concluding Remarks

Finally, though the points made in this is gloomy, it needs to be mentioned that most of those points are valid and relevant to the current state of the world. Therefore, without concerted action by policymakers and the citizens of the world, we are headed in the path of ruin. The fact that we have not inherited the earth, but have merely borrowed it from our children needs to be emphasized here.

United Nations Global Compact and its Implications for CSR Practice by Corporates

What is the United Nations Global Compact ?

The United Nations Global Compact is a set of principles that encourage the signatories to the compact to pursue social and environmental responsibility. Unlike the UN Millennium Development Goals, the UN Global Compact has corporates as its signatories and hence, this is the first comprehensive and cohesive CSR initiative by the UN that targets the corporates directly. There are many advantages of having the UN Global Compact, they relate to the fact that pursuing social, and environmental responsibility by corporates is easier to track and monitor. In other words, the UN has the mandate to monitor how well the signatories to the Global Compact are actualizing CSR in their everyday operations. Having said that it must be remembered that the UN Global Compact is not legally binding meaning that there is no legal obligation on the part of the signatories to actualize the targets set under the Compact. However, signing the UN Global Compact confers a certain responsibility on the corporates and it has been noticed over the last few years after the Compact came into existence that the corporates were indeed taking steps that would actualize the CSR objectives. Further, signing the UN Global Compact is like a badge of honor for the corporates as the partnership with the UN lends credibility and legitimacy to their CSR efforts.

The Principles of the UN Global Compact

The set of principles that make up the UN Global Compact include guidelines regarding social and environmental responsibility and range from setting aside budgets for CSR activities to taking on board the indigenous communities and those affected by the operations of the corporate in various locations around the world. In other words, the UN Global Compact specifies how all the stakeholders including the indigenous peoples, the civil society, and others must be brought on board by the corporates. Further, the UN Global Compact enjoins the corporates to commit themselves to protecting the environment, contributing to causes that are socially and environmental responsible, reducing emissions, and following best practices in their operations that would be CSR compliant. The key aspect about the UN Global Compact is that corporates have realized that signing it would add the much-needed legitimacy to their CSR activities and this has made many corporates especially the multinationals to become members of the compact. The case of the multinationals is particularly instructive as they operate across the world and hence, the UN Global Compact has specific provisions to regulate their operations.

Need for International Regulation and the Threat of Green Washing

Taking the cue from the UN Global Compact, many countries around the world have passed laws that specify how the CSR activities of the corporates are now legally binding. In other words, there are many countries where it is now legally binding for the corporates to follow certain norms including allocating a percentage of their profits to CSR activities. This is the case with India where the recently passed companies' bill explicitly sets out rules and regulations that specify how the CSR activities must be carried. Having said that, it needs to be remembered that while national laws and regulations play an important part in actualizing CSR, agreements like the UN Global Compact are especially relevant in this globalized world where multinationals straddle the globe and hence, international agreements like the compact are very relevant to ensure some compliance with CSR. Apart from this, there have been many suggestions that have been made by activists and NGOs to the UN to ensure that the signatories to the UN Global Compact are not indulging in Green Washing or the term used to describe commitment to CSR in words but not in action. This is the danger that any agreements like the UN Global Compact carry, as it is easy for the signatories to claim that they are pursuing CSR whereas in practice, they renege on their commitments.

United Nations Millennium Development Goals and their Implications for Corporates

What are the United Nations Millennium Development Goals?

The United Nations (UN) Millennium Development goals (MDGs) are a set of goals that were signed into an agreement with the member countries of the UN related to human development, eradication of poverty, providing access to basic services like food, shelter, and clean water to the underprivileged and poor people of the world. These goals though were not legally binding were supposed to bound the members together in pursuit of global humanitarian objectives. These goals were agreed upon in the year 2000 and have several implications for corporates in the practice of Corporate Social Responsibility (CSR) and the pursuit of socially and environmentally responsible business practices. The nature of these MDGs is such that the signatories must pursue the humanitarian objectives in conjunction with the other stakeholders in their countries like Non Governmental Organizations (NGOs), Civil Society, and the Corporates. Towards this end, they would have to allocate resources for the actualization of the MDGs and work in conjunction with the corporates to reach out to the underprivileged and the needy. This means that the corporates would have to discharge their duties as responsible corporate citizens and hence, must correspondingly adhere to the norms of the UN MDGs.

How the MDGs are funded?

The funding for the programs identified under the MDGs must be shared between the government and the other stakeholders and this means that the corporates would have to share some of the burden. However, as mentioned earlier, since these MDGs are not legally binding and represent a kind of directive principles of state policies wherein member countries are encouraged to pursue humanitarian goals and objectives, it has been the case that the targets set for the actualization of the goals which were in the years between 2010-'15 have not been fully met. Further, the global economic crisis of 2008 has dealt a blow to the funding of the MDGs by the members and the corporates as well. This has meant that the actualization of the humanitarian objectives has been postponed or left to a future date when the initial aims were to ensure that the targets would be met by 2015. Of course, this does not meant that no work has been done as is evident in the way several countries in Africa have benefited immensely because of the largesse showered on them by the Middle Eastern countries and China among others.

A Small Step for the Underprivileged

Though there are many who point to the fact that the funding from these countries was out of a motive for commercial interactions with these African countries, the fact remains that the practice of CSR is not entirely devoid of commercial considerations. Indeed, CSR works best when the corporates are incentivized to merge social and environmental responsibility with commerce. Further, the actualization of some MDGs related to provision of internet access, broadband, and communication facilities to the needy, and goals regarding education especially of girls are objectives that have been largely met. This has been done from a humanitarian point of view as well as the fact that such goals help the corporates in building and nurturing the workforce of the future. Therefore, the MDGs represent a significant step towards a better and just world and though there have been setbacks, the overall aims and objectives have remained in place meaning that both the member countries and the corporates in those countries have contributed to the effort. Apart from this, as is usually the case when the UN sets humanitarian objectives, the idea is for the richer countries and the large corporations to contribute more and hence, the actualization of the MDGs must be viewed in this perspective.

Finally, the point needs to be made that the actualization of the MDGs represents a small step for the recipients in their quest to attain living standards on par with the developed countries of the world.

Unethical Practices and Sweatshops in Developing Countries

The Phenomenon of Sweatshops

The global marketplace is driven by intense price competition as well as quality considerations. This means that those exporters who can offer quality at the lowest price often bag the orders from the global corporations like Nike, GAP, Apple, and other western multinationals who outsource their production to emerging markets. Since the exporters have to cut costs to actualize profits at the lower rates that are competitive, they often resort to making the workers work in abominable conditions along with paying them paltry sums of money as wages. This phenomenon has been termed as the rise of the sweatshop culture where workers in garment factories, chip making units, diamond polishing facilities, and factories of the global exporters work in conditions that take away safety and benefits. Indeed, the situation has become so critical that in recent months, there have been a spate of incidents in these sweatshops that have brought back the spotlight on them. Starting with the collapse of a building in a garment-making unit in Bangladesh, to outbreaks of violence in Apple product making factories in China, to organized violence in automobile factories in India, workers are increasingly turning their ire on these unethical practices and the perpetrators of these practices.

The Role of the Corporations, Exporters, Governments, and Consumers

Some of the blame for this situation obviously lies with the global exporters. However, governments and the governmental agencies in the emerging markets like the labor officers and the law enforcement personnel cannot escape their share of the blame. Though it is good to be competitive in the global arena, this competitiveness cannot come at the expense of compromises on safety and the health of the workforce. Further, the global exporters often point to the fact that if they do not deliver the volumes at low prices, other exporters in competitor countries would take the business away from them. While this defense is indeed valid and true to some extent, the larger point about the need for global exporters to forego some profits for the workers welfare cannot be ruled out. Moreover, the global corporations have to take some of the burden of ensuring that their products are made in safe and healthy work conditions. The consumers in the west are also stakeholders as their need for ever and more and more cheaper products is resulting in the creation of sweatshops around the world. To sum up, all stakeholders of the global manufacturing supply chain have to agree that they can do their bit to improve the conditions of the poor workers in sweatshops in developing and industrialized countries.

Steps to Mitigate the Problem

The steps to create safe and healthy conditions for the workers in emerging markets would include:

Better enforcement of the labor laws

Lobbying by activist and advocacy groups with the western governments to insist on their corporations to agree to voluntary and law mandated monitoring of their production facilities in Third world countries.

Finally, the **spreading of the awareness among global consumers** that the products that they think are cheap are indeed coming at the expense of the lives of millions of poor who cannot afford them anyway.

This means that all stakeholders have a part to play in this process. There is already a movement towards certification of the products consumed in the West as being labor friendly on the lines of the "Green" label that mark products made in an environmentally friendly manner. The point here is that whereas environmental responsibility has entered the global consciousness, social responsibility has still not steeped into the consumer mindset. This is partly because the Green movement has been successful in convincing consumers and warning them of the dangers of environmental destruction. Likewise, there is a need for activists and governments to persuade the corporations to adopt a label on their products, which indicates that the product has complied with social norms and worker welfare.

How Inclusive Development by Engaging All Stakeholders is Essential for CSR

Resistance to Global Corporations and their activities

In recent years, global corporations have realized that their activities across the developing countries are running into trouble because of fierce resistance from those indigenous peoples whose lands are being acquired by these global corporations as well as protests from civil society activists and environmentalists regarding concerns over the ecological impact of their operations. Indeed, the resistance to the activities of the global corporations has been so high that in some cases, they have been forced to withdraw from the countries as was evident in the case of the global aluminum maker, Vedanta, and the global steel maker, POSCO in India. In these cases, these corporations had to desist from their expansion as the locals along with activists protested vociferously against forcible land acquisition and the environmental impact of the operations of these global corporations. The situation could not be salvaged and helped even after active intervention by the government as the courts ruled in favor of the indigenous peoples and their rights over their land that was being acquired by the global corporations. These are some examples of such action that has been repeated elsewhere in the world.

Making Indigenous people Stakeholders

A possible solution to this imbroglio can be the global corporations making the indigenous people stakeholders in their activities by giving them a share in the global corporations. Further, the government can pass minority land holding laws that would ensure that the indigenous people are rehabilitated and made partners to the development of the country instead of being the victims of development. The point here is that by making the indigenous people stakeholders and partners in development instead of condemning them to be victims of development, inclusive and all round development can be actualized. This is the key point that emerges from the recent moves by the Indian government to foster inclusive development by passing legislation that would take the consent of the indigenous people mandatory before acquiring their lands. The spirit of the law is such that the percentage of the indigenous people whose lands are being acquired and who have to agree to the acquisition has been raised so that the majority of the indigenous people acquiesce with the process. Further, minority rights over the developmental process would ensure that their interests are being taken care of by the government and the global corporations.

Inclusive Development and avoiding the Victim Trap

The other solution to the vexed problem of resistance can be found in the global corporations ensuring that the indigenous peoples are taken care of through inclusive approaches to development. These can take the form of the global corporations providing employment in their factories to the indigenous peoples, helping them sustain their communities and families through funding the education of their children and helping family members with their jobs. Further, the global corporations can also build schools and hospitals as well as community recreational and community beneficial centers and facilities. All these steps would have the desired impact of engaging and including the indigenous people in the activities of the global corporations instead of making them hostile towards the global corporations and their activities. Finally, the global corporations can adopt green manufacturing and Processual methods that would minimize the impact of their operations on the sensitive ecology of the communities abutting their facilities, which is one of the key sticking points and points of contention as far as the global corporations and their activities, are concerned.

In short, the key objective here must be the term inclusive as opposed to exclusive where the former means that everyone prospers in development whereas the latter is towards enriching a few at the expense of the majority.

Why Managers need to Wake up to the Century of Declines and Scarcity

From the Era of Abundance to the Era of Scarcity

The era of abundance is over and we are entering an era of scarcity. Right from oil and minerals to water and food, every resource that we have used to power and drive our civilization to modernity and progress is in decline. This means that managers and business leaders must wake up to the century of declines and scarcities as well as shortages and plan their strategies accordingly. For instance, in many multinationals, the focus is now on cutting wasteful expenditure and focusing instead of conserving resources and efficiency. In other words,many corporates are now devising strategies where they prune their budgets for employee welfare and employee recreation as well as introduce measures that would make efficient use of resources. This has translated into a paradigm shift where the focus is on making the most of the available resources instead of burning up all the oil and consuming all the resources. Already, many companies have come up with measures that would decrease the rapid use of resources that was the norm earlier and are now asking their employees and managers to use resources judiciously and responsibly.

How Business Leaders and Managers can Embrace Efficiency, Innovation, and Productivity

The waking up to the century of declines also means that corporates and manufacturing companies in particular have to optimize their operational processes so that they extract more from the same quantity of resources being used. For instance, it is no longer the case that manufacturing companies can afford to waste precious resources in their processes without increasing the output from them. This is because unless there is more efficiency and productivity, the money spent on the resources increases because of the rising costs of raw materials, which eats into the profit margins as the inputs become more expensive. Therefore, these companies are introducing innovative and efficient methods of production where they get more bang for the buck or in other words, more output and better output per unit of input. Indeed, this is the only way for them to survive the coming declines in resources as otherwise they would be left with reduced and shrinking profit margins and a general tendency towards drifting away into the mediocre and the also ran companies. No wonder many companies are going the extra mile to reward innovators and those managers who make efficiency, innovativeness, and productivity their mission rather than those who indulge in wasteful and extravagant use of resources.

Transition to a Sustainable Paradigm

Further, the era of scarcity also means that the focus is on conservation and renewing the resources rather than merely using up all the resources. This can be seen in the way universities and educational institutions of higher learning are introducing courses on sustainability and environmental management as a means of inculcating the spirit of sustainable business practices among the upcoming generation. Moreover, the focus on sustainability and conservation has to be driven into the heads of all employees and this is where business leaders and managers with a clear and cohesive as well as coherent vision can help matters. In other words, the world is no longer, what it was used to in terms of resource and material usage and therefore, the message that we have to be realistic about resource use has to percolate from the top to all layers in the organizational hierarchy. The key challenge that would confront the business leaders of tomorrow is how to make to do with less and produce more and how to transition the current industrial paradigm into the 21st century one where judicious use of resources and more efficiency along with innovation and productivity are the buzzwords.

Concluding Thoughts

Finally, this aspect of scarcity impacts us at an individual level as well and as this focused on the business side of the issue, we would be discussing what all of us as responsible and functioning members of society can do to sustain our societies and leave something for the coming generations instead of using up all the resources for ourselves without a thought for the future.

The Fortune at the Bottom of the Pyramid: The Business Opportunity Description

What is the Bottom of the Pyramid and its Implications for Marketers

Marketers around the world are discovering that there is a fortune to be made by targeting their efforts at the Bottom Billion or those who are near the lower end of the income pyramid. This means that they can market specific products and brands to these customers who traditionally were served by local brands and other products from the unorganized industry. The term Fortune at the Bottom of the Pyramid has been coined by the noted management expert and author, C K Prahalad, and describes the business opportunity that marketers have if they are smart enough to target this segment. The targeting of brands and products like Sachet Shampoos and Mini Cola bottles appeals to this segment as they usually do not have the capacity to buy bigger sized products as their daily consumption is dictated by the wages that they get. In other words, this segment typically has the means to spend less than a Dollar or Two on each product and considering the vast size of the market in both the developed world and the emerging markets, the potential for profits is enormous.

Multinational Success Stories

For instance, in India, Unilever markets its brands in mini and micro sizes wherein the product is priced at ten rupees or less and this means that this bottom of the market can afford it. Further, Coca Cola has mini bottles that cost less than ten rupees making it affordable and within reach of this segment. Moreover, companies like Proctor and Gamble have also latched on to this segment by packaging and targeting products that are within the reach of this customer segment. The point here is that many of these customers aspire to buy products and consumer brands but are limited by the amount of money that they can spend. Therefore, by targeting them by specialized marketing and at the same time, not diluting the product can ensure that this consumer segment is tapped and the rich source of profits is leveraged. This is especially the case in emerging markets in Asia where there is a significant class of consumers in this category and as the examples cited above reveal, marketers can make good money by targeting this niche segment. Further, the fact that these emerging markets have significant rural populations means that marketers can go the extra distance and target these segments in rural areas to multiply their earning opportunities.

Social Responsibility and Social Entrepreneurship

Talking about reaching out to poor and rural consumers, it needs to be mentioned that apart from the profit making chances for such marketing, there is also the added advantage of actualizing social responsibility. For instance, the Nobel Laureate, Mohammed Yunus pioneered the microcredit revolution in Bangladesh by targeting rural women who had the potential to save and grow their businesses but did not have the means to access capital. By providing them with seed capital and small loans or the micro loans, Yunus ensured that these women fulfill their dreams of being financially independent and at the same time, be profitable in their businesses. Similarly, in India, the White Revolution or the game changing Amul brand of milk products revolutionized the production and distribution of milk products. This was done under the leadership of Varghese Kurien who ensured that the bottom of the pyramid is tapped for its profitability as well as a means of actualizing social responsibility. Apart from these, there are many more examples of social entrepreneurship in the Asian countries that resulted from visionaries like Yunus and Kurien realizing the importance of the bottom segment of the consumers and targeting them accordingly.

Concluding Thoughts

Finally, as we have discussed, both giant multinationals and social entrepreneurs can profit from targeting the bottom half of the consumer segment and these initiatives have lessons for the next generation of capitalists and entrepreneurs.

Stockholder Management vs. Stakeholder Management
The Dominant View: The Business of Business is Profits

Ever since the modern corporation took shape in the form that it is now, there has been an overriding consensus that the corporation exists to serve its shareholders or stockholders. The late legendary economist of the Chicago School, Milton Friedman remarked that the "responsibility of business is to make profits". He also added that the "business of business is profits" and hence, according to this school of thought, there can no two ways about where the priorities of the corporation and its managers or owners must lie. These priorities towards the shareholders and the stockholders meant that corporations for a long time did not consider any social or environmental impacts of their operations and instead, basely continued to insist that they were in business to make profits. This meant that the bottom line requirement for businesses was to make as much money as possible and to satisfy their shareholders and stockholders at the expense of all other interests. Indeed, many businesses did not even think about what are now known as stakeholders and instead, took many of them for granted. The thinking was that once a corporation attained a certain size and a measure of profitability, it could command respect from its constituents and hence, the primary objective was to grow as fast and as large as possible.

The Alternative View: Including Externalities

This state of affairs continued until the mid 1980s when there was a growing realization that the corporations and their pathological pursuit of profits meant that the environment was being impacted along with the social costs of uprooted communities and disadvantaged groups being affected the most. This led to the formation of many activist and advocacy groups who took it upon themselves to petition the courts, lobby the politicians, and protest against the unfair business practices of the corporations. Slowly, the term stakeholders were being used to denote the multiple constituents that a corporation has to manage instead of just its shareholders alone. Indeed, until the 1980s the environmental costs of business were simply written off as externalities that were outside of the costs that a product entailed. For instance, if a corporation was polluting the environment, the effects of the pollution were considered to be external to the cost of doing business and hence, the corporation was not liable to pay for them. However, this was contested by the social activists and the environmentalists who protested against the rapacious practices of corporations and demanded that these corporations be made to pay for the effect that they have were having socially and environmentally.

The Present Situation

If we turn to the present, it is evident that the effects of continuous and relentless growth are climate change, deforestation, loss of biodiversity, uprooted communities, and large-scale income inequalities. Therefore, the point here is that we have reached a situation where the corporations cannot go on in a business as usual mode as their actions have imposed such a cost on society that even its shareholders/stockholders have started to be alarmed. This is the reason why it is no longer fashionable to talk about stockholder management alone and the term stakeholder management has come into vogue. If we compare the perspectives on stockholders and stakeholders, we find that the former are all about money whereas the latter are the humane side of business coupled with money. This means that corporations cannot ignore the stakeholders in the same way they cannot cater to stockholders alone. This is the key aspect, which must be considered when talking about stockholder management and stakeholder management.

Business as Usual cannot be go on

As mentioned earlier, we are at a stage where we have imposed too much costs on the world with our paradigm of unrestrained growth and hence, the time has come where we talk about all stakeholders instead of just interests who own the company. In other words, we have to accommodate the concerns of all groups who have a stake in the operations and the success of an organization, which extend farther than monetary aspects alone. Further, we need to consider all people as stakeholders of our activities and not only those who are paid a dividend annually. Corporations have a social and environmental responsibility towards the former, which is ethical, humane, and just in the interests of humanity instead of being obsessed about profits and money alone. In this respect, the governments of several countries (including developing countries) have mandated that corporations must set aside a portion of their revenues towards CSR or Corporate Social Responsibility. This means that its stakeholders have to be paid a social and ethical in addition to environmental dividend, which is not monetary along with the monetary dividend they pay out to the stockholders.

Conclusion

Before concluding this, it must be noted that all of us feeling the impact of the social and environmental costs of doing business as usual. Hence, it is high time all of us as future corporate managers, working managers, and concerned citizens have to ensure that corporations for whom we would work in the future or working already have to manage stakeholders instead of stockholders alone. In conclusion, stakeholder management is the way forward and stockholder management cannot suffice anymore. Corporations do exist for profits but at the same time, they cannot ignore the loss of profits that the larger society foregoes because of their actions. Indeed, sometimes these losses may be more than the profits that corporations make.

What social report should be prepared to gain the satisfaction of shareholders?

But I think from my perspective to environmental issues, financial issues, particularly if used in conjunction with institutions that are particularly sensitive issues that they demonstrated. (Financial problems in the financial crisis that already exists) (Zhang & Hill, 1998).

Generally there are three approaches in corporate social responsibility concept that can be explained as follows: First of classical economic theory, theories of origin is. According to this concept and the company has only one goal to maximize profits and consequently maximize the shareholders wealth. This concept has so far been accepted and supported the effort to achieve the goal of ethical and legal framework exist. The second theory is presented in the 1970s and based on social goals related to bringing maximum benefit to be considered. According to this theory, corporate managers must make decisions that are between the rights of shareholders, employees, customers and the general public to create balance. The result should be a coalition and solidarity between the various interests and concerns, and this coalition is the only way the company from the Max to ensure long-term profits. This decision is necessary organization in order to maximize profits rather than trying to earn the profit level that is appropriate and will provide a good level of social goals. The results of their activities are considered. And organizational decisions based on those ways in which society creates more responsibility must be taken. On this basis, to achieve social and economic welfare based on the theory and May lead to decisions based mentality is not helpful to the community. The government's role as a determinant of power is remarkable. Lobbying the government may be done in three(OECD , 2005):Determine the social and illegal activities.) adopt rules and laws in order to limit the activities of the community itself had been useful, but without enforcement it is disadvantageous to the health community.) dealing with a series of activities that have social costs and negative effects on the community. As for the taxes to pay for damages to the community. The main purpose of such taxes to encourage companies to reduce the effects of such activities and control them. Azbhs about the nature of government regulation to solve social problems is characterized in that the definition of corporate social responsibility is very difficult.

Profits and social responsibility in companies: You can also profit companies, they operate in? Yes, sometimes the idea that companies are required to take interest and benefit of the way is fundamentally incorrect. Currently, large companies frequently claim that the financial goals are to think of social services.

Management Association and the United Nations, encourage companies to follow such a line. No wonder that this interesting idea has already attracted numerous people, because they benefit both companies' social responsibilities of the cases where private interests and public interests are equals, the idea of corporate social responsibility seems to be irrelevant. Companies to increase profits, the resort to do anything, will ultimately lead to increased social welfare, but on condition that the interests and welfare are in direct contrast, almost no recourse to social responsibility will result, because managers are reluctant interest in public affairs act against the interests of shareholders. Companies should private interests or public interests are the way in, they choose, but sometimes the situation is more difficult than a simple choice. When the interests and conflicts of interests are focusing on social responsibility, more effective measures to enhance social welfare will delay. Since companies are expected to provide a solution to deal with problems, real solutions are not ignored. Proper performance and profitability: For a better understanding of the concepts of private and public interests, the circumstances of which we have no contradiction with the interests and welfare. Consider the market for healthy foods. Fast market to attract customers who offering suggestions are important to your health choices such as salads and other benefits are many. Other companies with a focus on low fat foods, whole grains and other foods to the public interest, their income. Progress in various fields of social welfare because investors are successful.

Similarly, auto manufacturers to meet the needs of consumers and producers less fuel and benefit the environment, as well as numerous companies have benefited by increasing welfare and reducing energy consumption and costs, have found the frequency of the profit. But the motives and strategies, these are not social welfare. Healthy food and fuel for vehicles with less time for their manufacturers, with no benefit, not common. Many of the company until the energy value was not increased to this size did not matter to preserve energy. Until such companies are to benefit the community take steps towards their interests. Less effect on

changing the ways that social activists have emphasized. The goal is to increase profits, not the organization's commitment towards social responsibilities, but in such cases has been proven that the methods of social activities for the benefit of society. Unfortunately, the use of the opportunities presented by companies to social welfare and the interest is persona (Mcnamara, 1999).

Conclusions

Since the relationship between the social, political, environmental, economic, trade has been increasing, organizations are faced with new dynamism. The challenge facing organizations is that they need time to increase profitability and respond to new social expectations and the simultaneous administration of these two seemingly contradictory outcomes that require Develop practical strategies and has positive effects on society and on the organization's reach. Implementation of social responsibility in organizations, including the mechanisms and strategies are effective in this regard. In fact, many organizations in addition to their traditional tasks are required to perform other activities, the purpose of these activities, responding to the expectations of society and its organizations are referred to as social responsibility. In this period, effective management, the management of ideas within their organizations and to release the built environment and wider society thinks, Why not separate from society organizations can make their Society cannot continue without the organization. Corporate income and also long-term risk of future profit company, will oppose. Resorting to social responsibility, none of the above does not solve the problems of pressure from shareholders on a sustainable growth in profitability, will fix the problem and causing managers with incentives to replace incompetent managers are focusing on the long-term goals The company will compensate the damages. Choices(Richmond&Etal 2003). Otherwise, it would solve these problems long ago. The best example in this regard, it is industrial pollution. Manufacturers to reduce pollution, high cost of factory pay dividends. Poverty, another example is given.(Hess ,2001). Companies could pay higher wages to workers, lower costs for products, reduce poverty, in this case the losses were incurred. In such circumstances, regardless of whether managers should pay attention to their social role of corporate interests? Can assume that should happen, but in practice expect managers to focus solely on social responsibility. Duty and responsibility of managers to increase profits in the company's shareholders. Even if the directors of the company regardless of who is to benefit society, they will certainly lose their jobs, because shareholders, hiring managers that keep profits at the highest level possible. In such circumstances, the move towards the social responsibilities of management is in conflict because of the expected management task is in line with shareholder interests, directors should otherwise have to think of another job. Many companies in social responsibility not only speak and do virtually nothing and it is due to tactical called Green washing. (Which supporters claim are environmentally friendly).Managers of the company profits in order to lose Mamas No, actually impose tax on the shareholders and decide how to spend its own arbitrary will, and instead of the elected government officials are even on a small scale. Private companies are a different story. If the manager to raise social welfare is willing to accept lower profits, the shareholders should not impose such. The successful managers of public companies, private investors wishing to spend part of their charitable purposes, like many companies that has been active in charity work, but managers should not private companies using shareholder capital, realize their philanthropic goals. In fact, the majority shareholder, significant amounts of their incomes from investment spending to help charities, or other methods to help improve social welfare are. Of course this does not mean that companies are free regardless of social consequences following their huge profits.(Cherry, 1978). However, resorting to corporate social responsibility through effective balance between corporate profits Vnf not public. There Regulations: The best way to bring balance profit public benefit corporation and is The best way is to bind the organization. The government has the power to enforce rules and would no longer need to rely on people. But government regulation is not perfect and sometimes due to decreased cost and inefficiency welfare. Industrial groups to influence policy in ways that are mostly useless, used or intended use of the expensive resort to profitability. Public corruption, the situation is worse, plus, all the causes of government failure in developing countries due to weak and often corrupt governments worsened. Despite all the problems, governments, trade unions towards social responsibility, more effective role in support of their common interests. Observers and supporters: Civil society as observers and supporters, and provide an important role in imposing the kind of behavior is integrated into the social welfare is reduced. Types of nonprofit organizations and movements for a broad range of interests of different views of social, political, environmental, ethnic, social and cultural offer. For example, «Rainforest Action Network», an organization that often works in the field of environmental protection and natural resource consumption. The website mentioned that the campaign to increase public sensitivity towards the environment and consumers is that environmental degradation and stigma spot for U.S. companies to know and this nightmare is to accept responsibility liability policies are adopted to preserve the environment. This approach tries to convince managers that we are in the interests of the community, is quite different because in this case does not adversely affect the financial balance sheets. Generally, such a hypothesis is specified and cannot record it as a way to impose restrictions on the behavior of the main labor union presidents, especially in most developing countries that lack sufficient resources to the influence of civil society and people to the release shares are not sufficient. Its branches were: Another alternative is the creation of autonomous systems, but it is on the same forms of social responsibility strategy.

This means that investment firms are unlikely to benefit shareholders in the public interest. The system of regulations that the government will be and variable environmental conditions, reaction is more efficient. Emphasis on transparency, commitment and consistent with what people expect from the concerns of governmental laws and approaches to this system. Morph types responsible government to ensure autonomy, according to the standards. If the industry in order to be successful, government must intervene and to enforce its regulations. Financial estimates: Finally, other aspects such as social responsibility of business managers are charged. Only safe and effective for long-term decisions, impose penalties, such as regular supervision, taxes, criminal penalties and public embarrassment, for social behavior is unacceptable. Social responsibility theory of trade, which is only accepted by managers Bazkavty know when work is done correctly, it should focus on theprofit.

Conclusion:

Research has shown that managers tend to be limited to corporate social reporting in accordance with the shareholder wealth maximization should be used. Research has also shown that managers believe that social pressures are causing companies to respond ((O'Dwyer, 2005). Consistent with the rules seem to be companies that led to the development and delivery of appropriate social reports.